Seasons

Poems by Susan Torricellas
Illustrations by Amy (St. John) Glasson

ISBN: 978-1-962363-41-9 (sc)
ISBN: 978-1-962363-42-6 (e)

Rev. date: 12/11/2023

This book is specially dedicated to my son, Russ,
his wife Kelly, and my beautiful grandchildren, Colby,
Gia, Isabella, Brooks, Hudson, and Emma.

Love you always,
Grandmommy/Grandma

To my loving husband Bob,
who has shown me the beauty of nature.

CONTENTS

WINTER

SPRING

SUMMER

FALL

WINTER

Geese

I watched the geese today
Flying in formation
Across the thick clouded grey sky
So many flocks
Fliting here and there
I think they have lost their way
Are so confused by the weather
The birds don't know whether to go or stay

I watched the geese today
Flying overhead
Honking and flapping their wings
Wondering if its spring
So they will postpone that southern trip
And stay in this place Until Winter has its say And is here to stay!!!

Time for a Change

Six black buzzards soar high
Wings held wide
Light and free
Like a beautiful symphony
Crinkled leaves float down
Cover the soggy ground
Some are swept along
By the singing brook
And drift in silence
Like a peaceful song
Fluffy white clouds
Scatter across a pale blue sky
The wind says goodbye
To the last of the Butterflies
A chill is in the air
The lovely flowers
Shrivel and fall
Winter has come to call
Until next year
When spring tiptoes in
And splashes us
With a colorful grin!!!

Just for one day

Just for one day
I sit on the back porch
Looking out over the property
I see the creek
Clear water
Gently flowing over the rocks
So peaceful
Not like last week
Flooded waters
Ice and snow
The deep freeze
No where to go

Just for one day
The sun is heavenly on my face
Even God's little birds
Are singing a happy tune
Almost feels like June

Just for one day
The snow is gone
From the trees and lawn
The sky is so blue
Not a cloud in sight
It gives me hope
For a star filled night
Nature's blessings
Came our way
For just one day!!!

Snow Is a Coming

Since Monday afternoon
The news stations have
Talked about for hours
That a major snowstorm is on its way
Even though it hadn't even hit land as yet
And no one was getting wet
As usual the super markets
Are crowded as can be
And the gas stations are lined with cars
To fill er up before it runs out
And the hardware stores are busy
As people freak out
purchasing shovels and rock salt
Anti- freeze for the car
Everywhere you go "Neighbor to Neighbor"
Says "Are you ready for the snow"?
A foot or more is forecasted
But we will see
It could turn out like so many times before
Just a Weather man's decree!!!

No Snow Zone

There should be a sign
At the county line
A no snow zone
No ice slippery roads
Frozen trees
Winter do not come near
It all stops here
No more bad weather
No more runny noses
Or freezing toes
No more cars that will not start
Aching backs and sore calves
Can take a nap

There should be a sign
At the county line
No snow plows
Or electric companies
Allowed inside
Just blue skies
Warm soft breezes
Flowers galore
Whippoorwills singing
And trees of bright green
Let Spring in the door!!!

A chill was in the air

A chill was in the air
Yesterday,
Although sunny and bright.
So I wear my coat
To sit outside
Barely a sound
A dog barks in the distance
The Cows are still
Tucked in the barn
Trees are mainly bare
Even though Spring
Is almost near

A chill was in the air
Yesterday
Breezes ruffle my hair
I love to read and write
Sit outside Cabin fever
Sends me here!!!

Where Are The Cows?

Where are the cows today?
Do they sense bad weather?
Is on the way?

Where are the cows today?
The farmer's field is empty
Of fresh cut hay
I fear the cows are in to stay

Where are the cows today?
The grass is still green
The sun shines bright
A blue cloudless sky
In my sight
But who can say
Where are the cows today?

A Vision of Red

He sits there on my porch railing
All puffed out
Full of himself
One proud specimen
A splendid creature of nature
Striking contrast
To the pure white snow
Covering the ground below
He peaks at the bread crumbs
Quite a sight
A beautiful red cardinal delight
His gorgeous feathers span out
Fluffy and bold
Giving him warmth
In the snowy cold

He sits there on my porch railing
All puffed out
He turns his head from side to side
Looks for a Predator who hides
He glances my way
And off he flies
A bright red flash
Gliding across a white stark sky
Just a beautiful Red bird
Looking for a way to survive!!!

Thoughts of Spring

A cloud filled sky
Bright sun peeking out
Now and then
The soft sound of an airplane
Overhead Buzzards flying high
With wings spread wide
Birds chirp and sing
Two more weeks till spring!!!

Who Can Believe?

Who can believe it is Nov 2
The day is more like spring
Even though the leaves fall
And change colors
The hot sun
Warms us all

Who can believe it is Nov2
The creek shimmers
Giving off a magical glow
The flies are still around
Green grass surrounds
The flowers
that should be gone

Who can believe it is Nov 2
Blue skies
And fluffy white clouds
The birds sing a lovely melody
They hope this is just the beginning
And not the ending
Of beautiful weather

Buzzards

The Buzzards spread out
Their coal black wings
Drying their feathers
In the noon day sun P
erched on wooden stakes
Leftover from Summer's take
They sit still
Like frozen statues
Mannequins in a window display
Wing span at least 3feet
From end to end
They know how long to dry
And when to fly away!!!

The day before yesterday

I saw a ladybug on my windowpane
The Robins were hoping around
Across the soft moist ground

The day before yesterday
It looked like spring
Was on its way
Birds chirping in the trees
Would soon be building nests
The spring flowers
Ready to bloom

The day before yesterday
I saw a ladybug
On the windowpane
Yesterday morning
Frost covered the grass
Like a wet frozen top
Rain fell later on

What happened to spring?
I swear it was here
Already near?

Climate Change

Thunderstorms rage and lighting strikes
Tornadoes and hurricanes destroy
Snow storms cover cities and towns
Rain pours down
Floods surround
Lakes appear where none were before
Climate change is at our door

Ice melts in the artic shelf
Drought cause fires and destruction
To our forests and whole towns wiped out
The Amazon trees are now just burned to a crisp

Farmers cannot produce the crops they need
To feed a nation of human beings
Many have no way out
Thirst and starve
It is not a hoax or mirage
But a serious cause
To do so much more to activate a cure!!!
Climate change is at our door!!!

The Clouds

The clouds this evening
Swirl and gather
Like mounds of whip cream piled onto
A pale blue sky

The clouds this evening
Cover the universe
With fluffy cotton candy
Ready to bite

The clouds this evening
Watch the birds chirp and fly
Over the treetops to settle
And rest in their nest

The clouds this evening
Remind me of a million cotton balls
Forming a soft cozy blanket
To warm our beds
On a cold winter night
A sight that makes
Everything
Bright and light!!!

Snowy Snowy Day

Snowy Snowy day
Snuggled in under the blanket,
Nice and warm with
A hot cup of coffee on my stand
And of course my handsome man
To cuddle me again

Snowy Snowy day
Beautiful and breath taking view
From my window pane
A world of white;
Cold and windy outside
But so cozy inside
Snowy Snowy day
Can Spring be far away?

Here We are Again

Here we are again
The weather man says
Eight inches of snow
Schools are closed
And slippery roads
The Artic Vortex
Puts us in a deep freeze
Frost bitten fingers
And toes
Red burning cheeks
And the forever runny nose

Here we are again
Shovel the driveway
Aching back
Tired and wet Is it over yet?
Boots and scarves
Put on our gloves again
Will it ever end?

Here we are again
Waiting for spring
To come back again!!!

The Snow

The snow is a lovely scene
Admired from my window pane
A white wide oasis
Of smothered covered places

The snow is a lovely scene
Admired from my window pane
I watched the little sparrows
Flying all around
They peck on the partially bare ground
To find a bit to eat with their tiny pointed beaks

The snow is a lovely place
Admired from my window pane
Children build snow men and have
A snow ball fight
Playing outside until it is almost night

The snow is a lovely scene
Admired from my window pane
Sled riding down the hill
What a thrill
To come to the end
And start all over again

Lovely Snow

Lovely lovely snow
Bright and fresh
A morning delight
That fell over night

Lovely lovely snow
The bare trees
Twinkle and glisten
In a maze of sparkling white

Lovely lovely snow
Fluffy and light
Wet to the touch
Cold to the face and nose
Here I go
Shovel my way
Through the
Lovely lovely snow

Cows Gather

The cows gather in the farmer's field
Heads bent low they munch and crunch
The last of the delicious grass
Oblivious to the cold wet showers
Drenching them for hours

The cows gather in the farmer's field
Focused on one thing
Filling their empty bellies
Before the snow and ice
Covers their carpet of green
And winter is spent eating grain
From the silo
These placid creatures sleep and dream
Of sunshine and flowers!!!

SPRING

Sitting on the Porch

I sip a cup of tea
And gaze out over
The grass covered earth
Near the rippling creek
What a beautiful spring day
The birds are chirping
"Hurrah-Hurrah"
The mower sputters and grinds
Finally it roars to life
Ready to cut the crabgrass
And anything else that gets in its sight

I sip a cup of tea
The world is at last free
From the snow and ice
Torture of cold cheeks and toes
Icy roads and even colder winds that blow
Daffodils are starting to sprout
The broken limbs and branches
We pile high
Are ready for a bonfire tonight
Spring has come along
There is no doubt
Just in time to heal my spirit
Inside and out!!!

A Spring Storm

A spring storm can roll in fast and furious
The beautiful white fluffy clouds
We admired a while ago
Now as black as night
Thunder and lighting
Soon shows its forceful might
As the rain pours out of the heavens.
A torrent fills up the gutters
Making deep and muddy puddles

A spring storm can roll in fast and furious
But as much as we get annoyed by this weather
When the flowers bloom and the grass is dark green
We feel blessed that
Nature did her best
To leave us these precious treasures!!!

The Moon

It doesn't matter where you are
In this world
To gaze at a full moon
It fills our hearts
With happiness and light

It doesn't matter where you are
In this world
You may be high up in a skyscraper
Or standing on a sandy beach
Looking up at the sky
Staring out the window of a car passing by
Or gazing through a hospital pane
On the third floor Wherever you are
The Moon is made for all eyes
Out of reach
But beautiful and unique!!!

Time to Cut the Forsythia

It's time to cut the Forsythia,
And bring armfuls in the house
The Vases are lined up in a row
To show off the beautiful yellow color
And its first spring glow
The bushes are thick and wild
The tiny flowers spread out
All along the branches
Creating a splendid splash
To decorate the yard

It's time to cut the Forsythia,
Their golden glow
Is gone too soon
So enjoy these fanciful flowers
While they last!!!

Last Evening

Cows munching
On the grass
Leaves slightly blowing
In the breeze
Pink sky at twilight
Birds in flight
Nothing like a spring night

Cows meander
Down the hill
They seem to enjoy
The cool evening still
So calm and peaceful
They finally lay down
Bend their heads
On a carpet of grass
As they claim their beds

There is something about Spring

There is something about a blue sky
White fluffy clouds
Warm sun on your face
Always fills my space

There is something about a slight breeze
A creek flowing by
A bird chirping
From a tree up high
In the Spring
Always makes me sing

There is something about
New life new awakenings
Nature coming out
After a winter's night
It always makes me mend
From within!!!

When I sit by the Creek

When I sit by the creek
And watch the water
Ripple over the rocks
Make a bubbling sound
As it flows along
Remind me of a soft
Romantic song
It touches something inside of me
I feel like a young child again
Playful and free
The creek is home to me!!!

Pretty Little Flower

Pretty little flower
Growing straight and still
The wind will surely
Scatter your petals
All over the grassy hill

Pretty little flower
It is hard to be the only one
Sitting alone under the noonday sun
Be strong little flower
And soon there will be
Lots of other flowers
To keep you company!!!

Should I?

Should I jump
On the rocks
In the rippling brook
And let the cool water
Roll over my feet
Or run around the yard
Enjoy the cool grass
Moist between my toes
As I watch the Daisies grow

Should I sit
Quietly and listen
To the many sounds of spring
Hear the Sparrow sing
An airplane flying across the sky
The warm sun on my face
It is a wonderful lace
I am all alone in nature's home

While the sky

While the sky
Is still blue
And the sun shines bright
I will watch the jets
Streak across the sky green grass growing
And the Blue Jay fly

While the sky
Is still blue
And the sun shines bright
I will enjoy
The wind ruffling the trees
And the multicolored leaves
Scattered in the breeze

While the sky
Is still blue
And the sun shines bright
I will savor all the good things
Nature brings to delight!

Moo

I always say hello to the cows
They graze across the road from my house
And they line up near the fence
Look at me with big brown eyes
Some curiosity as to what or who I am

I watch them in the early morning
As they lumber from the barn
Following the leader in a unison line
They disappear on the other side
To munch and lie in the sun

Later in the day
The cows return to the otherwise
Of the hill
Follow the leader
Until she gets her fill

There is something peaceful
About a field of cows
Whose greatest pleasure
Is a sweet grassy knoll
And a kind soul
To lead them home
When the day is done!!!

The Lazy Creek

I sit on the bank
To watch the lazy creek
Slowly bubble and flow Over the rocks
The sun shimmers on the surface
The translucent water
Makes a path under the bridge
Pass the grazing cows in the field
And the farmer planting his crop

The lazy creek
Softly swirls
Around the bend
Alongside the houses
Sprinkled on the hillside
And children riding bikes
Down a country road

On it goes
Until it meets
With the Mighty Susquehanna
And all its force
It rolls by
The fishermen on their boats
Who throw in a line
To catch a big one

The lazy creek
Is swept through the currents
To complete his mission
And joins the Deep Blue Sea
That appears in the Distance!!!

Spring again

I can tell it is spring again
The grass is moist and green
And the plants are budding into flowers
After days of April showers

I can tell it is spring again
The strawberry patch needs kind
Gentle hands to clear a path
For the delicious fruit to last

I can tell it is spring again
Mr. Robin sits alone in the apple tree
A proud red breasted spectacle
Who enjoys the fat, juicy worm
He just plucked from the damp wet earth

I can tell it is spring again
Nature is coming alive
The Forsythia bush
Is starting to display its splashy yellow
Array of flowers
And the birds bask in
The early morning hours

I can tell it is spring again
My heart is like a fragrant flower
Ready to burst forth
And open my petals
To savor the sun, the sky and earth!!!

Listen to the Birds

Listen to the Birds
At twilight time
They sing and chirp
A Melodious sound
From high
A wise old owl Hoots
High in the trees

Listen to the Birds
At twilight time
As the warm sun
Sets behind the hill
Soothes my soul
Makes me whole
Nature settles down
Peace and Quiet
All around!!!

Blue Heron

I look out the back door
There he is standing on one leg
On the edge of our creek
Suddenly he spots a fish
And dives down
Then off he flies
To a nearby tree
Dining on this delicious treat

Blue Heron Blue Heron
What are you doing here?
The Susquehanna is a better place to stay
That is where you belong
Not on our narrow waterway
It is okay with me
If you stay awhile
I love to watch such a rare beautiful bird.
Stay as long as you like
If you fly away
I will bide my time
Until another day!!!

I Do Love Birds

I do love birds
As they perch on a branch
Chirping and tweeting
So many different sounds
Create a peace and calm

I do love Birds
With their wings spread wide
They fly across the sky
The nightingale
Who sings at twilight
Those who splash and take a bath
In the creek
Doves sitting side by side
Robins in the Spring
Lovely Red cardinals
Yellow finches
The Mocking bird
Blue Jays King of them all
Big and small
Buzzards who clean up our streets
Eagles and Hawks
Lovely white Swans
Geese that honk
Ducks that quack
Barn yard owls
That hoot in the night I do love

Birds Sea Gulls
Reminds us of a day at the beach
Blackbirds, Parakeets and Parrots
Cockatiels and Pelicans
So Many marvelous creatures
Birds every place
All over this wonderful Earth!!!

The Peace of Quiet

The Peace of Quiet
What does it mean?
Lively sparrows
Chirp and sing
A Robin hops across the lawn
Ready for spring

The Peace of Quiet
What does it mean?
The spirit feels calm
All worries
Pushed to gone
Sunbeams caress the face
Like a soft warm embrace

The Peace of Quiet
What does it mean?
a gentle breeze
Ruffles my bangs
Airplane engine hums
Far away in the nearly cloudless sky
No traffic or noisy highway
Just
The peace of quiet
In the countryside!!!

Seven Buzzards

Seven buzzards
Flying high
Across the blue, blue sky
Round and round
In circles
They search the ground
For something rotten
On which to pounce

Seven buzzards
Wings spread wide
Now I see them there
Right over the top of my chair
I look up in dread
Hoping something
Won't land on my head!!!

Daffodils

Daffodils
So fresh and bright
Lovely yellow flowers
Blooming in spring's early light

Daffodils
Line the country roadways
Pretty petals cover
The gardens of many homes and farms
Everyone loves
Their delicate charm
The last shiny color
Bursting forth,
With shades of evening
They fade from sight!!!

To Work Outside

It's great to work outside in the spring
I plant Geraniums Daisies
And a Bleeding Heart Bush
That will burst forth with buds of pink
I will cut the Rodadendras and fill vases
With fresh clear water
And arrange the bouquets
All over the place

It's great to work outside in the spring
Weed the pathway to the Gazebo
Wash the lawn furniture
Until the chairs sparkle and gleam
Smell the fresh air
Take a walk to the creek
I listen to the mocking bird sing
Watch the buzzards soar
With wide open wings
In the spring
Feel the gentle breezes
Rustle through the leaves
Spring oh lovely spring
You make my heart sing!!!

It's Finally Here

It's finally here
The weather is clear
The Daffodils and Crocus
Are starting to bud
The flies are lined up on the house
And stink bugs are coming out of the dirt and mud

It's finally here
A soft breeze ruffles my hair
As I sit on the glider
Just enjoying the scene
That lovely word
It makes my heart sing
Spring-Spring!!!

Through the Windowpane

I love to watch the rain
Through the windowpane
It whips across the sill
Like sheets of glass
It trickles down
Soaking the barren ground
I snuggle under the blankets dreaming
Of days long gone

I sleepily watch
The cars race through the puddles
So happy to see
The wet drops playing
Hide and seek with the trees

I love to watch the rain
Through my windowpane
It is fun to know
I am secure and dry
And cozy inside!!!

Rainstorm

It rained all night
A torrential down pour
Pound-Pound-Pound
On the roof
Waking me from sleep

It rained all night
Next morning
The road was flooded
So was the creek
The ground was already saturated
Mucky to walk on
The birds hid in the trees
The groundhog snuggles in his hole
They all wait for a break-
Which finally comes
With the ending of the rain!!!

A Thunderstorm is Coming

A thunderstorm is coming
The big bang is on its way
The lightning practices
For its grand display

The white fluffy clouds
Are turning black and gray
The blue sky says goodbye
To a sunny day
The awning flaps
In the wind
A tiny bird hangs on
To a broken limb

A thunderstorm is coming
The creek roars and churns
The leaves and debris
Buried in its depth
The signs are all around
The rain pours down in buckets
Covering the town!!!

Black Clouds

Black clouds gather
Thunder roars
Lighting strikes
The wind tears through the trees
They sway to and froe
Branches are ripped from limbs
Land on the ground
Scattered all around
Shingles fly
Groundhogs hide under the shed
Rabbits run full of dread
The countryside is alive
With falling debris
The telephone lines
Knocked aside
Lanterns come out
As we huddle together
Until the storm has passed
On its way south!!!

I Sit Along the Creek

I sit along the creek
In the brilliant warm sun
On a spring afternoon
That feels like summer
The music of the water
Flowing over the rocks
Creates a gentle sound of life anew
The frisky birds fly overhead
Then perch on a branch
To sing a happy tune

I sit along the creek
What a wonderful day
The Daffodils and Forsythia
Are in full bloom
The Lavender bushes are sprouting
From their winter nap
The grass is dark green
The world is a splendid place
Every creature is a part of this magical space
Without even knowing!!!

When the Day is done

When the day is done
And it is twilight time
I love to watch the stars come out
And the Moon appear
A huge golden sphere

When the day is done
And it is twilight time
I Love to breathe in the evening air
And marvel at the sunset
As it disappears

When the day is done
And it is twilight time
I feel the earth's gentle glow
And the eerie sounds
Of creatures big and small
Nature's night time calls

My Master Piece

If I could put in a bottle
The perfect nature's way
Keep it under glass
To admire and display
It would be this day

If I could put in a bottle
The brilliant warm sun
And capture the color of blue
On a fabulous tapestry
I would add the thick green trees
Waving in the breeze
It would be My Masterpiece
For all eternity!!!

So Quiet

So quiet out here
This evening
A little bird
Perches on a telephone line
Chirping softly
He looks into the distance
Full of pride
Just glad to be alive

So quiet out here
This evening Not even a breeze
Ruffling through the trees
Can invade
The still of a country side
Near twilight time

Beautiful Day

Beautiful Day
So sunny and bright
Blue skies and light white clouds
The kind of day
Just to be Alive

Beautiful Day
Mowers roar
And Airplanes soar
On their way
Pass heaven's door

Beautiful Day
Birds perch high
In the Sycamore trees
Singing
Tweet, tweet, tweet
To the summer like breeze!!!

Today is a lovely Day

Today is a lovely day
Sun shines bright
The clouds are
Thickening up
But still some blue left
In the sky
A slight breeze
Tickles the trees

Today is a lovely day
Not too warm
Or cool
Just enough to calm
The soul
Just enough
For nature to rule!!!

Beautiful Evening

Beautiful evening
Gentle night
Open up your lovely curtain
Display the end of Nature's Golden day

Beautiful Evening
Gentle night
Clouds of sparkling white
Hide the shadowed Moon
Until the stars shine bright

Beautiful Evening
Gentle night
Softly soothe
All Nature's creatures
Until the morning light!!!

All the little birds fly

All the little birds fly
Across the faded sky,
On tiny webbed feet
They softly perch
On limbs and twigs.
The Merry birds enjoy
The ending of the day
In a spring like way

All the little birds
Sing in unison
An orchestra of heavenly sounds
With a contented melody
They settle down.
On angel wings
They fall asleep!!!

The Little Bird

The little bird
Hangs on a limb
In the flowering pear tree
Chirping a lovely melody
I wish I knew what he was saying
Such a happy soulful sound
Maybe he is singing
It's spring it's spring
My nest is full of baby birdlings
And plenty of fat juicy worms around
To feed their hungry mouths"

The little bird
Hangs on a limb
In the flowering pear tree heart filled with pride
He sits with his chest puffed out
A heart filled with pride
Tweeting out loud
"It is great to be a bird"
Great to
Open up my wings
And fly"

Sing Little Songbird

Sing little songbird sing
Sing a happy song
Sing of lovely sunny days
And a glorious sunrise

Sing little songbird sing
Sing as you perch upon a limb
Sing until the sun slips
Behind the Mountain high
Sing to the mellow blue
Of heaven's skies
gentle breezes
And pretty flowers
As they Open up and grow

Sing of calm and peaceful evenings
Sing a happy song
The whole day long!!!

Evening

The evening sun
Sinks down behind the hill side
Sending rays of brilliant light
Across the pale blue sky
The cows graze in the nighttime shade
A white cloud drifts by
Shaped like a winged bird in flight
The nightingale sings from high
In the trees
A soulful lullaby
Two sparrows sit side by side
On the telephone line
The silence is a wonderful reprieve
A quiet song
From the world we live on!!!

Sitting on the Porch

I sip a cup of tea
And gaze out over
The grass covered earth
Near the rippling creek
What a beautiful spring day
The birds are chirping
"Hurrah- Hurrah"
The mower sputters and grinds
Finally it roars to life
Ready to cut the crabgrass
And anything else that gets
In its sight
I sip a cup of tea
The world is at last free
From the snow and ice
Torture of cold cheeks and toes
Icy roads and even colder winds that blow
Daffodils are starting to sprout
The broken limbs and branches
We pile high
Gathered for a bonfire tonight
Spring has come along
There is no doubt
Just in time
To heal my spirit
Inside and out!!!

SUMMER

Beautiful Clear Day

Beautiful clear Day
Blue sky
Not a cloud in sight
Slight breeze flows
Through the trees
A yellow finch has his fill
Of sunflower seeds in the bird feeder
Cows graze contently on the hill
Birds are chirping happily
This is the kind of day
Makes one glad to be alive
Surrounded by nature
And all its glory
So grateful to be outside!!!

Summer Storm

The thunder rumbles
In the distance
Warning of another
Storm on the way
The clouds are as black
As a Halloween cat
And the lightning strikes
Across the sky
Almost touching the treetops
Flash of fire lines streak by
Making the day
As dark as night

The thunder rumbles In the distance
Warning of another
Storm on the way
Stay inside and hide
From this scary sight
Until this summer fright
Has its say!!!

Pink and Blue

Pink and blue sky
White quarter moon
In a twilight night
Birds zip by
Lightning bugs
Flash and dance
Across the lawn
Cicadas are back
With their eerie sounds
Serene silence
Covers all
Evening in the countryside!!!

Swinging on my Glider

Swinging on my glider
In the noon day sun
I try to find a shady spot
To hide behind
As the wind ruffles
Through the trees
I listen to the birds
As they chirp and sing
The butterflies land on the railing
Display their multicolored Angel wings

Swinging on my glider
In the noon day sun
I see the buzzards soar across the sky
They spread their wings and dip down
Looking for a tasty treat that is rotten
And ready to eat
I hear the mower roaring up and down
My Husband's on a mission
To get it done
Before the night time comes!!!

Morning Shade

I came out to sit on my porch
In the Morning shade
Before the sun beats down
Over the green, green ground
I could not believe
A white half moon
Could still be seen
In a cloud less blue sky
Yellow butterflies flit
Here and there
The cicadas sing in unison
A melodious song
Birds chip
Snuggled high in the treetops
Cows lumber down the hill
Munch on grass
In the morning still
A slight breeze
Ruffles my hair
A kind of peace
Fills the air

The Rambling Brook

How soothing and calm
The rambling brook sounds
As it flows on its way
Over the jagged rocks
Pass the cows and farmland
Through the dense forests
Under the bridges
Saying "Hi" to the children
That splash and play in its cool wetness
They laugh and squeal
As they tiptoe
Over the slippery rocks
The fishermen enjoy casting into the water
Looking for the big one

The countryside disappears here and there
The brook ripples pass the trees
Reflects sunbeams
It reappears down the line
Just a rambling brook
As happy as can be
Until he reaches the deep blue sea!!!

The Gardener

If you see him with his large straw hat
Dirty work boots
Bare arms red from the sun
Old rough work gloves
Worn from years of use
He will have a shovel in his hands
You will see the gardener
Ready to plant

If you see him with sweat
Pouring down his weather beaten face
It is the gardener
Tying up and putting stakes around
Tomato plants
He places onion sets in a row
Deep in the fertilized and limed ground
Prepared months ago
The yellow squash vines have spread out
And peppers are dark green
Sweet enough to eat

There he is the gardener
On the hill watering his crop
He has a careful plan
The end result
Producing a bountiful crop
He gathers red juicy tomatoes
Bright yellow squash
Delicious scallions
And giant butternut squash
Bending the vines
The gardener
Already knows
You reap what you sow!!!

The Gazebo

The Gazebo is a wonderful peaceful space

To sit and contemplate
A respite from the hot sun
An evening Oasis when day is done

The Gazebo is surrounded by green bushes
And fragrant flowers
A gentle rolling creek
Drifts over the rocks in the distance
White clouds float by in a blue summer sky

The Gazebo is a special refuge
It's a magic spot
I must say
My girl cave
I sip a cold drink
And think of how lovely the day is
How great to be alive
In this place and time!

A Day well Spent

What a way to spend a sunny day
Swimming in the Conowingo pool
I relax on the lounge
And watch the sleepy Susquehanna
Flow by
As buzzards fly high

The wind whips through
A mass of dark green trees
The blue sky overhead
Unfurls shapely white clouds
I imagine one looks like a small dog
Chasing a chicken with wings flapping
Maybe the big angry mass
Could be a fierce dragon breathing fire

What a way to spend a warm sunny day
My man and I play around
In the cold refreshing water
Hug and splash each other
Once we have had enough
Of a day in the sun
We pack up and go home
Looking forward to our return

Natures Room

Relax a little
I tell myself
Let the mind unwind
Watch the creek flow slowly
Over the rocks
Be mesmerized by the dance
Of the Dragon flies
Just relax
And feel revived

Relax a little
I tell myself
Like a statue on the shelf
Quiet and still
No cell phones loud music
T.V. screen ringing in my ears

Relax a little
I tell myself
Just sit back in my lawn chair
I close my eyes
And feel the soft air
Caress my hair

Relax I say to myself
Remember what it feels like
To be covered with peace
Complete silence inside
And no gloom or doom
Outside
In natures Room

To the Creek Again

Down to the creek again

Back to breathe
Away from cabin fever
To peace and tranquility

Down to the creek again
Where Breezes blow
And the water gently flows
Birds sing a happy melody
I feel revived and free!!!

I Sit by the Creek

I sit by the creek
Listen to the birds chirp
Watch the water swirl
Over the rocks
And across the muddy bottom
The cows are grazing in the thick green grass
Hot summer sun
Beating down on their backs

I sit by the creek
Under the shady pear tree
Read my book
And write a little poetry
Tiger lilies thrive all around
As white lace flowers
Line the banks
Nature aplenty
On this fourth of July 2020

Ramble On 04/19/16

Ramble on bubbling creek
Swirl and spin.
Around the bend
Under the bridge you flow
Tiptoe through the wooded glen

Ramble on bubbling creek
Twist and turn
O'er slippery rocks
And broken twigs-
A home for tiny minnow fish

Ramble on bubbling creek
Pass the bank where bumble bees hive
And butterflies thrive
Where children dip their feet inside
As you zip by
They splash and play
Then send you on your way

Ramble on bubbling creek
Don't look back
At where you have been
Just hurry on
For the mighty Susquehanna waits
For you in the end!!!

I sit in the Quiet

I sit in the Quiet
In Nature's room
Barely a sound is heard
Except one single bird
A faint buzz of bees
Swarm the clover leaves
It is a place of gorgeous flowers
Giant trees grow lush and green
A peaceful scene

I sit in the Quiet
Of Nature's room
On the bank of a lazy stream
Sparkling with sunbeams
As I gaze at the pale blue sky
Fluffy white clouds drift by
And I imagine
I am in a Dream!!!

The Rambling Brook

How soothing and calm
The Rambling Brook sounds
As it flows on its way
Over the jagged rocks
Pass the Cows and farm land
Through the dense forests
Under the Bridges
Saying "HI" to the children
That splash and play in its cool wetness
Laughing and squealing as they tiptoe
Over the slippery rocks, jumping from one to another
The fishermen enjoy casting out
In its deeper depths for the big one

How soothing and calm
The Rambling brook
As it meanders along
The Country side
Disappearing here and there
Rippling through the trees
Reflecting sun beams
It re appears
Down the line
Just a Rambling Brook
As happy as can be, to reach the deep blue Sea

A Summer Afternoon

A woodpecker pecks the huge oak tree
He drills into the wood
Looks for a juicy insect to eat
A tiny sparrow splashes
And drinks from the creek
He loves the cool wet
Flowing over his feathers
Bumble bees savor the clover
Suck the nectar
Flowers open up their petals
Enjoy the warm sun
Birds chirp and sing a happy tune
On a hot summer afternoon!!!

Summer Afternoon

As the soft breeze
Flows over your face
You open your eyes
To marvel
At the sparkling creek
Drifting by
This is when your spirit
Comes to life

Nature is the place
To listen to the birds
Chirp and tweet
And find your inner peace
Under the shade of a Magnolia tree
You are light and free!!!

Black clouds

Black clouds
Mar the beautiful red sunset
Blocking out the golden sun

Black clouds
Cover the blue
Turning the world
Into a frightening hue
Thunder and lighting
Appear on the horizon

Black clouds
Force the rain from the sky
Buckets pour down
Causing every creature to hide

After the Snow

After the snow
A white wonderland appears
Untouched by animal paws
Or human hands

After the snow
The sparkle blinds
The eyes
And this unmatched beauty
Makes you feel alive

After the snow
The scene is serene
A kind of peaceful sight
Sent from above
To cover the night
With a unbelievable
Tapestry of white!!!

What Happened?

What happened to the sunny days?
And warm gentle twilights
The rain came down
Out of the heavens
Like a huge faucet
It caused floods rivers overflowed
Damp messy days and storm filled nights

What happened to the sunny days?
The kind that encourages flowers
And thick green grass to grow
Tomato plants to reach high
Toward the hot summer sky
The rain covered the ground
And caused a huge mucky mess
The seeds I planted today
Just floated away
Mother nature swooped in
That was the end!!!

Daytime says Goodbye

The cows are mewing
In the fields
The evening air
Soft and still
An airplane engine roars
Overhead
As all the world
Is put to bed

The cicadas
Create an eerie melody
High in the thick
Green trees

The sky fades
From bright red
To pale pink
And golden yellow
As it sinks
Behind the hillside
Daytime says Goodbye

When Evening Comes to Call

When evening comes to call
And the sun slowly sinks in the sky
As time gently slips away,
Songbirds sing their lovely lullaby
I fill up with a sense of peace
Soon quiet rules my soul
Work and play are done
Flowers close their fragrant buds
And all the creatures of the earth
Find a special spot to snuggle at night

When evening comes to call
I listen to the silence
Welcoming the twilight
As I contemplate my life!!!

Quiet Tonight

It is so quiet tonight
All I hear
Is the cicadas
Singing in the trees

It is so quiet tonight
The birds have flown to their nests
And nature slowly rests

It is so quiet tonight
The last rays of sun
Color the sky
The Moon waits near by

It is so quiet tonight
The cows are long since gone
Not a sound remains of the day
Just a jet plane far away

It is so quiet tonight
I wrap my blanket tight
As the world folds up
Until the morning light!!!

It Is A Cool Evening

It is a cool evening
We have had so few of those
It is either hot or humid
Or a cloudy rainy night
Without the moon and stars
To bring us
Heaven's light
The sticky sweaty mess
Has disappeared
And gentle breezes fill the atmosphere
Lovely calm air washes
All the world with care

It is a cool evening
A long time coming
Let us hope it stays
And lingers on
Until the Dawn!!!

So Quiet

So quiet out here
This evening
A little bird
Perches on a telephone line
Chirping softly
He looks into the distance
Full of pride
Just glad to be alive

So quiet out here
This evening
Not even a breeze
Ruffling through the trees
Can invade
The still of a country side
Near twilight time

Full White Moon

Full white Moon
Way up high
In the pale blue sky
Soon surrounded by a million stars
An illuminating sight

Full white Moon
Way up high
In a pale blue sky
The sun still shines bright
As it slips behind the mountain side

Full white Moon
In a pale blue sky
Slowly says goodbye
To the daytime hour
The sounds of life
And welcomes the sounds
Of a black black night!!!

Little Bird

What are you saying Little Bird?
As you chirp and twitter away

What are you saying little bird
Does it mean
You are so happy today
To be alive in this twilight time

What are you saying little bird?
Do the other Birds understand
And return your musical song
With a chirping of their own

What are you saying little Bird?
Come light upon my hand
And let me listen
And softly talk to you
From a human point of view!

She Flew In

She flew in
A dainty female
Cardinal She hopped from limb to limb
Colored by God's hand
A soft Red Rose
Lovely to behold

She flew in
Swiftly with wings opened wide
So close I could almost touch
Her silken side
But then she suddenly surmised
That I was quite alive
And Boy did she fly!!!

Follow the Leader

The cows are really herd animals
I watched them this evening
As they saundered across the rim of the hill
One behind the other
The lead cow stopped suddenly
And the others followed suit
Almost banging into each other
Not one tried to move out of line
And come on the side of the hill
Where there was plenty of grass
To graze on

I have seen it before
If one cow romps down the hill
The whole herd follows
If one meanders to the creek
Her buddies go right after her It is amazing to see
If one cow looks at me
When I say" hello ladies"
They all lift their heads
And listen out of curiosity!!!

LITTLE Birds

Little Birds
Wings spread wide You soar
Way up high
Across the earth and sky
I wish I could be with you
And see what you see
Valleys of green, Rows of corn, Reds and yellow of trees
Flowers in bloom
Gone too soon

Little Birds
Avoid the scorned ground
Fires illuminating cities and towns
Unhealthy maze of smoke and haze
Filling the air all around

Little Birds
There soon will be
No where to live
With this environment
No where to build your nests
Or settle down to rest

Little Birds
It breaks my heart
This climate change It is wrecking havoc
In our world
These creatures have no where to hide
No way to survive
Sadly it is getting worse and worse!!!

FALL

The Creek

You can look at a creek
From far away
And it is just
A body of water flowing on its way
But pull up a chair
And really sit and stare
It becomes a rippling brook
Rolling over the jutted rocks
Bubbling and swirling
And curling along
Singing a spring time song

You can look at a creek
From far away
It is just a
Body of water flowing on its way
Pull up a chair
On a sunny day
Watch the little fish swim and play
Notice the Butterflies in the butterfly bush
And the tiny birds building their nest
This is nature at its best

This is the Time

This is the time for Pumpkin picking
Carving out a Jack a lantern
A child's delight
Apple dunking and delicious cider donuts to try
Add scrumptious pie

This is the time to keep black cats
From crossing our path
Halloween night of witches and fairies
Super heroes and freaks so scary
They roam our neighborhood streets
It is the time for trick or treat

This is the time for warm days
And clear cool nights
Beautiful colored Mums
To plant for next
Fall Time for leaves on every tree
To turn red- yellow and orange
Enjoy the season before winter comes to call-
This is the time
For Fall!!!

Fall Is

Fall is clear cool mornings
Warm afternoons
Blue skies =Pumpkin pies
Fields of Mums
As high as the sky

Fall is gathering
The last tomatoes
Clinging to the vine
Trimming trees
Red-yellow and orangs
Bright turning leaves
A lovely season to savor
Chat with a neighbor
Farm shows craft fairs
Festivals and garage sales

Fall is school days -school plays
Fun filled field trips
Hay rides and apple pickings
Apple butter thick and de-lish"
Pumpkin chunkin
Halloween munchin
It is Geese flying in formation
Honking their horns
To advise the nation
To look for the signs Winter is not far behind!!!

October

October is a month of different seasons
Frost in the morning
Coats the car windows
And grass with a shiny white hue
Blue skies and afternoon sun warms
A light breeze makes it feel like spring
Cool nights announce
It is Fall again

October a month of different seasons
Pumpkins covered the vines
Beside the last bloom of summer flowers
They try to hold onto their brilliant colors
Until the cold wind makes them shrivel
And forced to say goodbye

October a month of different seasons
The trees display colors of orange yellow red and brown
Send a shower of discarded leaves
To the ground.
Can winter be far behind?

I Watch the Creek

I watch the creek
Reminds me of a gentle lullaby
So soothing and serene
Like a lovely country scene

I watch the creek
Little ripples sparkle In the bright sunlight
Over the rocks the water
Ebbs along
Like an inspiring love song!!!

Listen to the Quiet

It is so quiet out here
I swear I can hear
The slow beating of my heart
Even the birds
Who fly from tree to tree
Seldom make a sound
I hear the faint bark of a dog
Far off in the distance
And I finally start to rest
Forget the worries
Piled up in my head

It is so quiet out here
The silence
Soothes my soul
Caresses the whole
Human core
I feel a kind of peace
Only felt
At Heavens door!!!

I Love Fall

I Love Fall
Warm Days
Chilly nights
Pale blue, cloudless skies
Full harvest Moon
Stars sparkling bright

I Love Fall
The season of apples
Apple cider
Pumpkins and Pumpkin pie
Craft fairs farm shows
Funnel cakes and ice cream shakes
Football again
And Homecoming games

I Love Fall
Colorful Mums
Red, yellow, golden leaves
Decorate the trees

I Love Fall
Snuggling together
Bring out the jackets
Turtle neck sweaters
For the cool breezy weather

Fall Hovers Near

A jet streaks across the sky
Leaving a flume of white
The golden sun
Sinks behind the hill
Late evening
End of summer still

A dog barks in the distance
Creatures call
As twilight falls

The leaves dance around
Cover the ground
With yellow and brown
A change is in the air
Fall hovers near!!!

Fall

Fall is nipping at my bare legs
As I sit and swing on my glider
There is a chill to the air
Cool and clear and so invigorating

Fall is an evening of peace
pale blue sky and a quarter
Moon standing by
Fall makes being outside worth
All the hot summer haze
Ad humid sweaty days

Fall is a prelude to winter
Leaves turn gold, red, yellow
Then float to the ground
Bare trees all around

Fall is Fairs, flea markets, farm shows
Auctions and beautiful colored Mums
Pumpkins orange and bright
Ready for fresh Pumpkin pies
And scary Jack A Lantern Nights

Fall is getting to be
My favorite time to see!!!

A Hand from Above

So many clouds
Piled high
Under a pale blue sky
Fluffy and white
Like a million cotton balls
Soft and light
I feel the warmth of the sun
Covered with a cuddly blanket
Relaxed and free
Birds swarm to the feeder
Red Cardinals Sparrows and Doves
A day touched
A hand from above

It is Time for the BlueJays

It is time for the Bluejays
Those black ringed blackeyed bandits
Who swoop in for the kill
All other birds beware
The Bluejays are here Five fly in
And cover the ground
Turn the birdfeeder almost upside down
Beautiful birds it is true
But they seem to demonstrate
They are King of the hill
In Nature's plan
They are head of the clan!!!

(A Change is in the Air)

The butternut squash
Are ripe and ready for harvest
Bright orange
Pumpkins Weigh down
Twisted trailing vines

The last of the tomatoes
Are picked
From yellow plants

Rows of onions
Dry in the cool sunny morn

Corn stalks shrivel
And bend in the wind

The freezer is packed
Full of this year's bounty

A change is in the air
Hot humid haze disappears

Cool crisp clear Breathe in the clear smell
Autumn is here!!!

Beautiful Sight

Such a Beautiful sight
Streaks of red
Decorate the sky
The sun sinks down
Behind the color splashed sky
Cows bend their heads
To graze
For the last delicious bite
On the grassy hill
The twilight appears
All is still

Such a Beautiful sight
Birds softly chirp
A special song
Cicadas begin an eerie sound
As Fall moves
Right in!!!

What is Boring?

Someone said to me
"How is boring Peach Bottom"?
Boring I replied?
I love to watch the cows
Grazing in the grass
And the Amish framer plow the fields
Boring?
The many colorful birds that eat the sunflower seeds
In my back yard
Red headed woodpecker Bluejays sparrows
Yellow finches
Robins in the Spring

Boring?
These are Natures gifts
A beautiful scene
The flowing creek
Where I write my poetry
Bumble Bees and Hawks
A country walk
An Amish horse drawn buggy
Clip clopping down the road
Rabbits and Groundhogs green frogs
And a lumpy old toad
A wide open sky
Alight with the Moon and Stars
Boring? No Way!!!

www.ingramcontent.com/pod-product-compliance
Lightning Source LLC
Chambersburg PA
CBHW081001120626
46546CB00010B/2990